Furious Triangle

Furious Triangle

Catherine Vidler

PUNCHER & WATTMANN

First published in 2011

Published by Puncher and Wattmann
PO Box 441
Glebe NSW 2037

http://www.puncherandwattmann.com

puncherandwattmann@bigpond.com

National Library of Australia
Cataloguing-in-Publication entry:

Vidler, Catherine

Furious Triangle

ISBN   9781921450310

I. Title.

A821.3

Cover design by Matthew Holt

Printed by McPhersons Printing Group

This project has been assisted by the Australian Government through the Australia Council, its arts funding and advisory body.

Australian Government

Australia Council
for the Arts

For Nick, Oliver and Jeremy

Contents

Stars   9

No stars tonight   10

Counting the stars   11

Stars   12

No stars tonight   13

Counting the stars   14

20 one-word poems   15

Three wishes   16

Caught in the storm   17

Contradiction   18

King Kong   19

10 two-word poems   20

queue poem   21

19 lines from Lund   22

Proportions   23

Outside, inside   24

Botanic Gardens, Sydney   26

At Taronga Zoo   27

Balmoral   28

The oval   29

Bushwalk   30

13 Canberra rondelets   31

Beyond the tense tapestry   36

12 New Zealand snapshots   38

Wellington   39

Feeding the birds   40

9 signs of terrestrial intelligence   41

Untitled   42

Three unfinished fairytales   43

Villanelle   44

Five poems I didn't write   45

Ernie and Bert sestina   46

Diminishing poem   48

Warbling poem   51

love poem   52

Upside-down poem   53

Orange orchard   54

Golf course   55

After the circus   58

Haunted sestina   63

Source code poems   65

Eye chart   68

Source code for The Asterisk Machine Mark 3   69

Collaborations with the Google Poetry Robot   72

Notes   78

Acknowledgments   79

Stars

The sky is nothing

but a spray of stars,
tiny consolations.

Under the buttery stars
Oh,

they are a frozen swarm
of thoughts

(the night's not mine)

and so much wishing
to be done.

No stars tonight

No stars tonight,

cloud only,
only cloud.

*

The steaming river
is upside down,

a stun of star-fish
clings

to its hidden
floor.

*

But something more,
(I overlooked)

the darkness,

strung
like an old guitar

or a boat;

supple, fantastic, afloat.

Counting the stars

Nothing left to do but count
the stars

(I could be here all night).

*

Like stopped confetti

their utterances
reside, bright-lipped

round the moon's
pale head

(the abacus has gone to bed).

*

Oh chuckling stars
what can I do

but cut my losses
and count on you.

Stars

5: define SF_CENTER 1 # Star at center of image
   define SF_MARK1   2 # Mark stars in first image
   define SF_MARKALL 3 # Mark stars in all images

*

338: // Consume any number of stars.
       while ((c = in.read()) == '*')

No stars tonight

26: //set the background to no stars
     echo "<ul class=\"star-rating\">\n";

*

93: c = *pattern;
     /* Collapse multiple stars. */
     while (c == '*')

*

30: if ($rating->rating == '-1') {
     echo "<li class=\"zero-stars\"><span

Counting the stars

558: my $self = shift;
     my $count = $self->stars();
     $self->stars($count - 1) if $count >

*

43: //1 star 1 1 to 12
     //2 stars 25 13 to 37
     //3 stars 50 38 to 62
     //4 stars 75 63 to 86
     //5 stars 99 87 to 99

0;

*

446: * int score
     * score in 'number of stars'
     * [MAX NUMBER OF STARS DECLARED IN CONFIG FILE]

20 one-word poems

no*r*m

w*rest*le

indivi*dual*

*n*od

tri*but*e

camou*flag*e

w*hole*

exqu*isit*e

inter*mi*ttent

*enter*p*rise*

*revel*ation

*over*tone

s*afar*i

*dim*inish

free*whee*l

h*ear*

hea*ring*

colou*red*

rem*ember*

foo*two*rk

15

Three wishes

wis*he*s
wis*he*s
wis*he*s

Caught in the storm

th*under*cloud
thunder*cloud*

Contradiction

fals*if*ied
au*the*ntic

King Kong

skyscr*ape*r

10 two-word poems

ellips(is land)mass

va(st ar)dent

fini(sh ine)ffable

gra(sp ill)usory

fla(sh immer)sion

bri(sk y)awning

enli(ven n)exus

ventu(re ad)venture

id(le af)lutter

lea(f *in*d)ex

que

19 lines from Lund

1. Crocuses break through the grass like truants from a fairytale.
2. Birds warp the sky in slow swerves, starbursts.
3. A skating rink adjusts its size to the landscape.
4. Cloud strokes a cold pool of sky.
5. Crates of shopfront tulips paint the light.
6. The Cathedral is a storm in an arch blue sky.
7. Flowers ring the feet of trees, fooling winter.
8. The sky is a cobalt coat of arms.
9. Precise birds swirl in a corridor of dusk.
10. Cathedral sandstone renders the sky in overcasts of darkness, cloud.
11. The unearthed cobblestone is a rubik's cube solved in granite.
12. Rain muddies the gravel's usual routines.
13. Rotund pines squat out the winter with ever-green confidence.
14. The Cathedral wears the moon at a jaunty angle.
15. Snow tracks the decisions of tree trunks, branches.
16. A pot-plant sends its small warmth across the courtyard.
17. A cloud of birds kneads the brisk evening sky.
18. Bracing streets, powdered with early light.
19. Brief trees begin to elaborate.

Proportions

Stone bowls,

inflated to the size of small ponds, their brims shimmering with flowers. I see them waiting at intersections, walking the streets, at the square, high in the air, everywhere...

Crows

Each one holds an invisible magnifying glass, and won't be seen without it.

Jurassic Park

Under the sensible deciduous tree, prehistory shrinks to a point of view. Dew trembles upon the intricacies of a jungle: teeming tree-ferns, over-sized flowers, clearings, pungent mud. It goes for miles and miles. I gaze down through a chaos in the canopy, searching for Brachiosaurus, the biggest of them all.

Street lamps

Suspended over rivers and creeks of swirling cobblestone, they are like miniature cable-cars stopped mid-flight, letting light admire the view.

Winter trees,

enormous burrs, catching at the clouds.

Spring shrub

Like fish in a coral from The Giant Reef, yellow flowers collect in its branches, sway in gentle currents, catch the sunlight.

Outside, inside

Inside the dining room window, 2 April, 2008, evening

A wall-hanging hangs on the wall where the clock was stopped before. Two sneakers stand at right angles to their socks. In the doorway to the lounge room, a chair has stepped away from the computer to assess the situation in the dining room.

Outside the dining room window, 13 February 2008, dawn

The sky lightens in almost imperceptible increments. The mouth and ear of the scaffolding slowly sharpen in silhouette. Only the outer top portion of the birch is visible, tangling a piece of sky between two buildings.

Inside the dining room window, 10 February 2008, morning

The clock is stopped at 10 past 10. The door to the kitchen rests ajar. A pile of clothes gathers all the disorder in the room and gives it a voice. A light hangs from the ceiling like a dark-pink luminous lolly, precisely processed.

Outside the dining room window, 14 February 2008, pre-dawn

One lamp lights only itself.

Outside the dining room window, 10 February 2008, morning

A winter birch waves gently. Some scaffolding peers over the roof of a building. Five black birds fast out-run the clouds. Awnings jut and curve over dark brown doors in the opposite apartments. On top of a roof made of grey-metal panels stacked like a card-house, a small satellite dish turns outward like an ear.

Inside the dining room window, 7 April 2008, afternoon

A coffee table waits next to the wall, open-palmed. Drawer knobs are reflected in the white sheen of their host drawers. A bag of miscellany laughs on top of the chest of drawers. Tissues hang listless from the top of a box of Kleenex.

On the dining table, neon straws are more or less lined up in a plastic packet illustrated with two straws (red and yellow) sitting in a glass of water.

Outside the dining room window, 26 April, 2008, morning

The birch is beaded with lemon-lime leaves. Its top branches are slightly animated. The scaffolding noses up to the central chimney of the opposite building. The left-most chimney also bends towards the central chimney. Pink blossoms make puffy dots at the edges of spring shrubs outside the opposite apartments. The sky is a panel of light grey.

Botanic Gardens, Sydney

Under the Chinese elm,

a quivering kaleidoscope
of light and shade.

Cryptogams, communicating

in alternative languages,
beyond flowers.

Poppies, cupfuls of trembling

light, stems bending under
a rainbow's weight.

Bats, hanging from trees,

strange fruit, self-wrapped,
always in season.

The harbour sails by,

a magic carpet, glittering
in the wind.

An ibis eyes a crust.

The sudden cutlery
of its beak.

At Taronga Zoo

1. Echidna quills filter the wind.
2. A free-ranging emu is overly familiar.
3. A tortoise moves like a secret.
4. The viscous seal pool trembles with anticipation.
5. A cable-car sags like a burdened planet.
6. A submerged crocodile turns, its tail a slow goodbye.
7. The carp pond is brimming with silver and gold.
8. A barn-owl flashes its white heart at the crowd.
9. Koalas warm the eucalypts' joints.
10. A peacock reserves the right to party.
11. Zebras calmly stand their ground.
12. Hunched chimps concentrate the heat.
13. Wallabies loll like an indulgent audience.
14. Harbour views continue to unwrap their surprises.

Balmoral

Boats crowd the mouth of the bay

      like teeth

         like things waiting to be said.

The water is brown and breaking up

           like biscuits in a shaken jar

      like resolve.

The oval is soaked

      like a giant bath mat

         like an overwritten manuscript.

Clouds unbalance the sky

           like a conspiracy theory

      like standing on one leg.

Personal trainers unpack their routines

      like reverse origami

           like new years' resolutions.

Cockatoos rip up the grass

      like cockatoos rip up the sky

         like nothing else.

The oval

Foliage marches backwards
from the margins, colluding
like a language

under steep blue sky. Clouds
are scattered, inert zooms,
swallowed whole by light.

The sun, a sheer massive,
poises on the edge of its seat,
missing nothing.

*

The oval is frayed, like a worn
drum. Arrhythmias feast
on its surface, strung out

to curvatures; path, road
and luminous swells of park
before the bay's bold

brochure, thrust with boats,
receding into fine-print
energies; ripple, glint, breeze.

Bushwalk

The giant flowering shade.
The absence of flowers.
*

The aerated spectrum of green.
The stadia of articulate leaves.
*

Light, stumbling down the slope.
Light, bouncing off the gully floor.
Light, settling semi-height.
*

The lucent sapling.
The lucid sapling.
*

The loose mesmerism of the track.
*

Boulders, held in suspense of their falls.
Boulders, holding their histories intact.
*

Lichen's tight-knit rounds of turbulence.
*

The egalitarian moss.
The demonstrative moss.
The green moss.
The orange moss.
*

Trunks (their winter coats of bark).
Trunks (their winter coats thrown off).
*

Reflective creek.
*

The clear-eyed caves.
*

Roots, clenching to a sheer of rock.

13 Canberra rondelets

1.

Here is the shade.
In a field, a tree's small statement.
Here is the shade.
In a landscape of erasures,
rubbed surfaces; a fire-work's
frozen flower, its shade thrown down.
Here is the shade.

2.

The bright foaming
grasses, the co-existence of
the bright foaming
cloud, the sparse aquarium of
sky, a liquorice twist of tree.
A street-lamp stoops. In lieu of grass,
the bright foaming.

3.

Parliament house
lands, a UFO. Clouds alight.
Parliament house.
Clouds alight over soft-poured hills.
Trees offer sparse bouquets of shade.
A hedge makes a break for freedom.
Parliament house.

4.

Trees, quivering,
anticipate the coming storm.
Trees quivering.
Sculptures sculpt surrounding spaces.
Willows teem on a rolling creek.
Bull-ants, etch-a-sketching the dust.
Trees, quivering.

5.

Lily-pads shine,
serve exquisite floral desserts.
Lily-pads shine
in the strong afternoon light like
polished saucers on gleaming cloth.
Carp shelter in the shade beneath.
Lily-pads shine.

6.

A galaxy
of flowers, sustained by a shrub.
A galaxy.
Terrains of shade maintain their space.
Between the gums, birds flitting like
insects, insects flying like birds.
A galaxy.

7.

A sculpture wrings
moisture from the late afternoon.
A sculpture wrings.
Parrots pester the dozing grass.
A statue contemplates the pond;
perpetual carp, the water.
A sculpture wrings.

8.

The sandstone church,
standing in the foreground. Behind
the sandstone church,
Parliament house, rising. I think
of a sparrow at the foot of
a gull. Supple roads swirl outward.
The sandstone church.

9.

Leaves, coins flipping.
Fountains collapse like wedding cakes.
Leaves, coins flipping.
The Lake's vacant gaze, broken
by breeze, occasional boats. A lake
like a visitor, always here.
Leaves, coins flipping.

10.

Overcast lake,
like a melted cloud, downcast. The
overcast lake
rolls out its long thirst. Throughout a
tree, gumnuts scatter like tiny
compliments. Canberra stretches.
Overcast lake.

11.

Intricate edge
of the lake. Its blank centre, its
intricate edge.
Two swans trailing our paddle-boat.
Vegetation, delving into
details. A nest entwines itself.
Intricate edge.

12.

Cubicle hedge.
A sculpture's sudden metaphor.
Cubicle hedge.
Sculptures, rearranging space like
furniture, or puzzle pieces.
Dusk leaves gleam like stars in reverse.
Cubical hedge.

13.

Two park benches.
A sculpture with a perfect view.
Two park benches.
On a wall, ivy suddenly
stops, like a broken fairytale.
The wattle is a froth of white.
Two park benches.

Beyond the tense tapestry,

leaves were alive
with light,

water's bright
chaos came

in shards
and clouds, nauseous

with possibilities,
pushed on regardless.

*

From the ground, bark
considered

its countlessness;

so much to deal with,
so much time,

while further down,

at a chipped tooth
of shore,

two dandelions lifted
their fists

to the wind.

*

All around, that day
fell apart

like cards,

like a house, collapsed,
making way

for the stars.

12 New Zealand snapshots

1.   A spent river makes minor calculations: curve, distance.
2.   Cows eat fast air from the edge of a ravine.
3.   Bamboozled tussocks hold their blades erect.
4.   Cabbage trees dream of the dinosaurs.
5.   The sky is scuffed with cloud.
6.   The cloud is scuffed with light.
7.   White Rock, a man from outer space.
8.   Leaves whipped into seizures of rumour.
9.   The land, a swept jigsaw of horizontals, verticals.
10. Roots clamp onto the dirt like frightened spiders.
11. A milky sea, flavoured with sky.
12. Emerging birds, stitches in the clouds.

Wellington

Gifted clouds,
a moonscape bay,

gulls levering
the baffled sky.

I lived here once,
under a text of stars,

wind tearing up
all my translations.

Feeding the birds

At first when we arrived there were none there.
The muddy slope, unpromising, the lake
a perspex wall tossed down, a stare,
as full of content as an empty rake.
We pulled the bag out from another bag.
Unpromising, its content barely there,
enthusiastic as a sagging flag,
(we must have missed the first beads of a stare).
At once the slope was righted, birds were dice
and playing-figures tossed across a board.
We held position in a mental vice,
encircled by the ornamental horde.
It was the bag that overcame the fray:
Now empty, it put all the birds away.

9 signs of terrestrial intelligence

Gum leaves shower their branches with shimmering insights.
Sea-snails to an unknown power colonise the rock.
Rock oysters gawk in all directions.
Dandelions insist on defying gravity.
A palm's fronds, mesmerised by cloud.
Lichen wakes a beast from its garden boulder.
Tidal sand quickens its wits.
Storm water twirls towards the solution.
Trees realise the wind with shivering acuity.

Untitled

Bunched vapours cross,
pungent with instinct.
The rain, falling like code,
erases yesterday's equations,
tries again.

Cars drool over the crest,
starry-eyed, the revelation
of road almost too dark
to bear (a roundabout collapses
in its moat of drone).

Mushrooms blaze the outskirts
with a wild language,
beyond consumption.
Night permutes into anagrams
of steam and star.

Data smarters, in the dark
the moon plays ping-pong
with the clouds, and this old man
can see the future in a head of garlic,
twirled between his fingers.

Dazzled, I return to the window.
Google is lifting the net
on a storm of question-marks,
and everything new
is old again.

Words colonise the clouds.
The sky grows dark with wings.

Three unfinished fairytales

1.

She is untying a bow.
Air trembles round her fingers.
The clock has arched its back.

Her hands are pulling the world apart,
yet the ribbon grows longer, longer,
longer still...

2.

The meal is cold.
Outside, a clod stirs in sympathy,
turns its body to the window...

3.

Upstairs is a bed
made of tiny umbrellas.

One by one, they are opening.

The room is swelling
with cupped air and polka dots.

Still they are opening, one by one.

The house clutches its side.
Will no one stop them?

Villanelle

Amongst cool pastels and clean-lined cement,
champagne flutes delicately effervesce
(the towering ghost-gum is its own event).

Hors d'oeuvres arrive, configurate, present
themselves to tables with acute finesse,
amongst cool pastels and clean-lined cement.

Synthetic music opens like a tent
of longings with no permanent address
(the towering ghost-gum is its own event).

The room begins to rhyme as guests invent
new ways to coincide and coalesce
amongst cool pastels and clean-lined cement.

Plants' potted extroversions complement
the steady deck, this sky's a perfect mess
(the towering ghost-gum is its own event).

Lawn falls and interlocks like a relent-
ing world, a game of chess, a lucky guess.
Amongst cool pastels and clean-lined cement,
the towering ghost-gum is its own event.

Five poems I didn't write

1. This is the poem I didn't write about a group of nuns waiting for fish and chips. Coalescing, drifting apart, coalescing again. Petals of a sea-anemone. The shop was an aquarium of heat.

2. This is the poem I didn't write about childbirth. 1. Broken waters. 2. Howling tree. 3. Keillands forceps (the wandering method).

3. This is the poem I didn't write about fifteen non-grammatical uses of the word "if".

4. This is the poem I didn't write about a corporate gift basket: Golf balls. Mixed nuts. My best friend bursting out of a mini.

5. This is the poem I didn't write about photo booths. A series of likenesses is located beside the phones. Will only say "photo". Your complete privacy is cut short by the curtains.

Ernie and Bert sestina

"Let's see," says Ernie.
He wonders if he should wake up Bert.
Bert is reading the newspaper.
Ernie interrupts. Pigeons in the window!
Ernie eats one of Bert's cookies
and leaves, holding Bert's umbrella.

Bert attempts to go under Ernie's umbrella.
This wakes Bert up. Bert complains to Ernie
but there are still four cookies.
Ernie suggests singing a lullaby to Bert.
Everything is wet. It's raining and a window
is stuck open. Bert gives up reading the newspaper.

Ernie asks his question: can he borrow the newspaper?
Ernie, however, has only brought an umbrella.
He opens a window,
and a statue starts tapping and talking to Ernie,
drawing the same reactions from Bert.
Cookie Monster appears. "Do you have any cookies?"

Ernie says he doesn't have any cookies.
Through binoculars, he can see Bert reading the newspaper.
Ernie imagines what life would be like without Bert.
It turns out that Ernie has Bert's umbrella.
"Bye-bye!" says the statue, and laughs…just like Ernie.
Sherlock Hemlock helps Ernie find out how his window

got broken. Ernie looks out the window.
It's Mr Snuffleupagus! Ernie replies that he has no cookies
and therefore the apple belongs to Ernie.
Ernie refuses to take his turn to go for the newspaper.
He pushes Bert away from the umbrella,
struggling to save a plate of cookies for Bert.

Mr Hooper and Tom serve sodas to Ernie and Bert.
When Bert looks out the window
Snuffy is gone. Ernie brings an umbrella
but Bert doesn't want to see four cookies.
Ernie talks to Rubber Duckie until Bert is done reading the
newspaper.
"No, I wouldn't. I'd think it was funny!" says Ernie.

Snuffy appears, opening the umbrella for Bert
as Ernie tries to close the window.
If only the cookies would stop putting crumbs in the newspaper!

Diminishing poem

making something
smaller or less
important or becoming
smaller or less
important or appearing
smaller or making
something appear
smaller or tapering
or making something
taper from the lower
part to the upper part
or becoming or making
something smaller
in size or amount
especially gradually
or narrowing the
shape of something
like fainting light
for example from
a small candle.

*

making something
smaller or less
smaller or less
smaller or making
smaller or tapering
taper from the lower
part to the upper part
something smaller
in size or amount
especially gradually
or narrowing the
shape of something
like fainting light
a small candle.

48

*

smaller or less
smaller or less
smaller or making
smaller or tapering
taper from the lower
part to the upper part
something smaller
especially gradually
like fainting light
a small candle.

*

smaller or less
smaller or less
smaller or tapering
part to the upper part
something smaller
like fainting light
a small candle.

*

smaller or less
smaller or tapering
part to the upper part
something smaller
a small candle.

*

smaller or tapering
part to the upper part
something smaller
a small candle.

*

smaller or tapering
part to the upper part
something smaller

*

smaller or tapering
part to the upper part

*

part to the upper part

Warbling poem

pre-performance warble
pre-performance warble
pre-performance warble
pre-performance warble

performance warble

pre-performance warble
pre-performance warble
pre-performance warble
pre-performance warble

love poem

this is
a poem
about
a dream

about a
dream
about a
poem.

he dreamt
he dreamt
he was
a poem

slipped in
between
her sleeping
lips so

when she
woke she
spoke his
name.

Upside-down poem

The ivy was profuse,
torrential even.

But it bit so lightly
of the expectant

air, and it didn't
need to know why,

it was there.

Orange orchard

Beyond here, there might
be an orange orchard.

Each tree a kind of orchard.
Each orange eating the sun.

Golf course

and fade,

and loft,

and green fringe,
and successive wind.

And come
and walk
the spill,

and flush
the lacing
birds.

And pool
begin,

and humbling

arrival.

Miracle.

Circuitous driftage,
shape,

and spin,

and flunk stream
tendencies.

Trace, navigate,   wriggle,

yaw

                  and

        roll

     about meander shape.

                Detour prescience,
                voyage bite

                and finish

swerve.

          Oblique roam
            (blockaded coast),

       layer,

            lode,

                    middle of the road.

                Gallery glide,
                time

                and tide

and hopscotch ooze.

                    (Float sailing,
                    skim enclosure,

     fairy's brink
     and catalogue corner)

                    Channel
                apostrophe

                                        tail-wind

        turn,

                                          and veering turn.

                Mark swing, carry slalom string.

Wild align.

                                          Zany beeline.

                Curricular groove, and planetary,

side-dish whirl south-westerly.

                        Stray narration, speculate.

                                        Preternatural
                        inflection.

                        Starting gate...

After the circus

Anagram 1

Caped in faded glitter
at 8 pm, rotund,
the elephant slept.
Caped in faded glitter,
here, on trodden popcorn,
ears muddied like tricks,
real as the music.

Folding its wings,
in a tent of large dreams,
the elephant slept.

Umbrella to the stars,
sky falling like scarves,
ears muddied like tricks,
real as the music.

Anagram 2

At 8 pm, rotund,
folding its wings,
the elephant slept.

Real as the music,
umbrella to the stars,
sky falling like scarves,
the elephant slept
in a tent of large dreams,
caped in faded glitter.

Caped in faded glitter,
here, on trodden popcorn,

ears muddied like tricks,
ears muddied like tricks!
real as the music.

Anagram 3

Caped in faded glitter,
umbrella to the stars,
the elephant slept.
Ears muddied like tricks,
real as the music.

Caped in faded glitter,
here, on trodden popcorn
in a tent of large dreams,
ears muddied like tricks,
folding its wings.

Sky falling like scarves,
the elephant slept
at 8 pm, rotund,
real as the music.

Anagram 4

At 8 pm, rotund,

caped in faded glitter,
real as the music,
umbrella to the stars,
the elephant slept.
Caped in faded glitter,
here, on trodden popcorn,
ears muddied like tricks,
sky falling like scarves.

Real as the music,
ears muddied like tricks.
Folding its wings
in a tent of large dreams,
the elephant slept.

Anagram 5

Caped in faded glitter,
real as the music,
at 8 pm, rotund,
folding its wings,
the elephant slept
in a tent of large dreams.
Ears muddied like tricks,
real as the music.

Caped in faded glitter,
here, on trodden popcorn,
umbrella to the stars,
the elephant slept.
Ears muddied like tricks,
sky falling like scarves.

Anagram 6

Folding its wings,
ears muddied like tricks,
at 8 pm, rotund
the elephant slept,
sky falling like scarves.

In a tent of large dreams,
the elephant slept,
caped in faded glitter,

here, on trodden popcorn.

Caped in faded glitter,
umbrella to the stars,
real as the music.
Ears muddied like tricks,
real as the music.

Anagram 7

Folding its wings,
ears muddied like tricks,
the elephant slept,
caped in faded glitter,
here, on trodden popcorn.

At 8 pm, rotund,
sky falling like scarves.

Real as the music,
ears muddied like tricks,
caped in faded glitter.
Real as the music,
umbrella to the stars,
in a tent of large dreams,
the elephant slept.

After the circus

At 8 pm, rotund,
folding its wings,
the elephant slept.
Ears muddied like tricks,
real as the music.

The elephant slept
here, on trodden popcorn,
ears muddied like tricks.

Caped in faded glitter,
in a tent of large dreams
real as the music.
Caped in faded glitter,
umbrella to the stars,
sky falling like scarves...

Haunted sestina

Haunted sestina beckons but offers no exit.
Spooky how a line can be so like a corridor,
words a conservatory of cobwebs,
rhythm a heartbeat knocking at the door.
The dining room table is long and dusty, its party
ages like a portrait, and isn't it spooky

how the grandfather clock has a voice, spooky
how poems don't always let you leave, the exit
drowned out by the organ's merry waltz, the party
dancing down an endless corridor,
obscuring the door,
the attic window blinded by cobwebs.

Where have all the spiders gone? Cobwebs
hang in the air like a chill, like spooky
bouquets, they're crowding the door,
and where is the exit?
An unseen person cries down the corridor:
This poem is a hall of mirrors, a party

with no guest of honour, a party
littered with deceased meanings, cobwebs...
Candles burn their predictions into the wall, the corridor
grins with amusement, it's spooky
how paper alone can disable an exit
and whoever heard of a house with no door?

Ghosts cluster like metaphors, clouding the door,
the cellar is swollen with monstrous memories, the party
refrains from discussing the exit.
Madam unfetters her tresses of cobwebs,
her crystal ball swarms with allusions, it's spooky
how poems are traps made for unwary words, the corridor

echoes the rap of her fingers, the corridor
shakes like a terrified door.
Lightning flashes, the reading begins with a clap, so spooky,
dead poets are risen and felled. The party
collapses, the clock tolls thirteen, countless cobwebs
weave poetry over the exit:

Haunted sestina, a party of cobwebs,
Haunted sestina, no exit, no door,
Haunted sestina, spooky corridor.

Source code poems

23: # \<option>joke\</option>
    # \<option>poem\</option>
    # \</select>

1: def poem(jumper, jumpee="moon"):
        out = [ ]

274: public void addPoem() {

7: 'poe', 'poeg', 'poegg', 'poegs', 'poen', 'poenj', 'poenh', 'poed', 'poel',
'poelg', 'poelm', 'poelb', 'poels', 'poelt', 'poelp', 'poelh','poem', 'poeb',
'poebs', 'poes', 'poess', 'poeng', 'poej', 'poec', 'poek', 'poet', 'poep', 'poeh',
'pyo', 'pyog', 'pyogg', 'pyogs','pyon', 'pyonj', 'pyonh', 'pyod', 'pyol',
'pyolg', 'pyolm', 'pyolb', 'pyols', 'pyolt', 'pyolp', 'pyolh', 'pyom', 'pyob',
'pyobs', 'pyos',

61: else
        echo \\<h3\\>Sorry, the poem doesn\\'t exist yet\\!\\</h3\\>
      fi

28: ;;
    ;; Body of poem
    ;;

74: poem   db   __n
            db   "this is not a nasty bug",__n

123: 'poem': poem,
     'song': poem,

'riddle': poem,
1075: // Chatbot-Alpha 1.7 - A reply with continuation...
    + tell me a poem
-       Little Miss Muffet,\n

98: u"grocery list", u"gift ideas", u"life goals", u"fantastic recipe", u"garden plans", u"funny joke", u"story idea", u"poem"]

472: /// <remarks>
    /// A poem
    ///</remarks>

33: EVER_ON_AND_ON
    say "Here's your poem:\n\n$poem";

539: poem: item
    sdesc = "paper"
    noun = 'paper' 'poem'

77: (require 'poe)
        (require 'poem))))

2409: pocketbook
    poem
    point

796: "plus",
    "poem",
    "poet",

208: POEM(1) := 'Mary';
    POEM(2) := 'had';
    POEM(3) := 'a';
    POEM(4) := 'little';
    POEM(5) := 'lamb';

15: #
    # To use, put some text between <poem></poem> tags
    #

362: "this looks almost l"
        "ike a poem but not.";
        const char *errmsg;

5637: (Laughs) You want my poem? Is that what you're asking for?
        [Quotes:]

298: /*
        * ca: I can't think of anything that would be appropriate here,
except a poem
        *

13: This is a fake poem
This is a fake poem
This is a
fake poem
This is a fake poem

54: /* When anything at all happens, make a new poem   */ public
void actionPerformed(ActionEvent ev) {

Eye chart

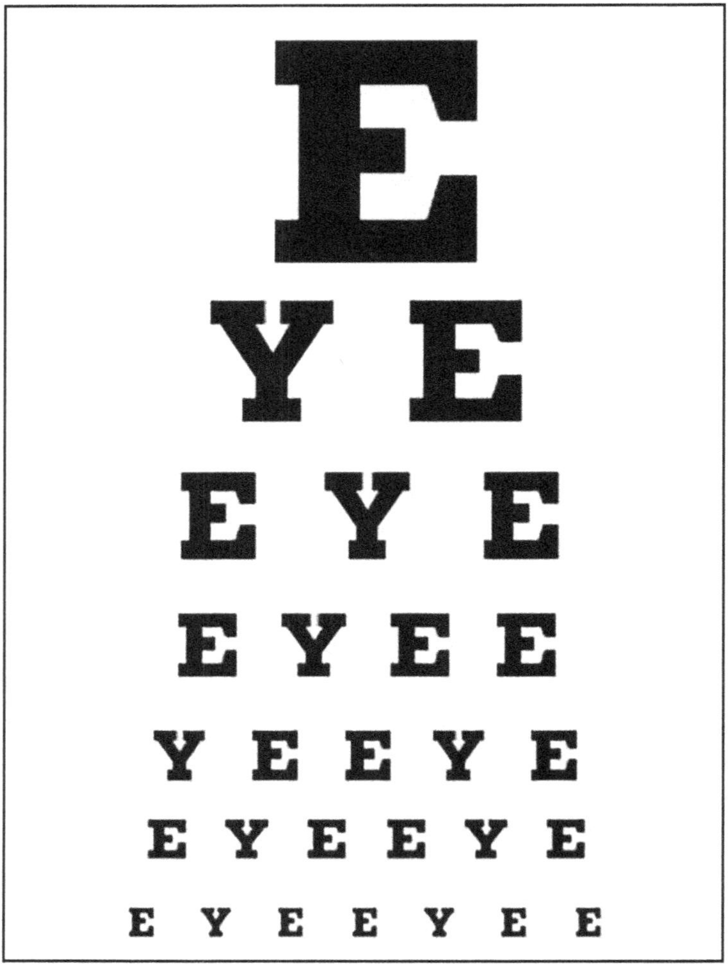
E
Y E
E Y E
E Y E E
Y E E Y E
E Y E E Y E
E Y E E Y E E

Source code for the Asterisk Machine Mark 3

309:    objectclass (1.3.6.1.4.1.10098.1.2.3.15 NAME 'goFonQueue' SUP top
AUXILIARY
    DESC 'Queue definitions for asterisk machines (v1.0)'
       MUST (cn)

757:    word(addictive, 430, 11).
    word('adding-machine', 431, 0).
    word('adding-machines', 431, 0).

3953:   word(asterisk, 2316, 1).
    word(asterisks, 2316, 3).
    word(asterisked, 2317, 0).

303:    objectclass (1.3.6.1.4.1.10098.1.2.3.14 NAME 'goFonMacro' SUP top
STRUCTURAL
    DESC 'Macro definitions for asterisk machines (v1.0)'
       MUST (cn)

850:    /*   */
    /* An asterisk (*) denotes a vertex whose identity is unknown.   */
*/

99: ;;; This matcher does not currently understand question   marks
  ;;; but understands multiple asterisks.

1062:   * the line is typed, but there is rarely anything to be read in
    * these cases anyway. (Wouldn't it be fun to display asterisks?)

1004:   int type = t.getType();
    // search for any combination of code and asterisks

138:    bool   m_multiline;
    /// show asterisks instead of actual characters
    bool   m_password;

445:    +   +   /* --- Deal with multiple asterisks. --- */
    +   while (wild[1] == '*') wild++;

4138: for (i = 0; i < numprompts; i++) {
        /* 32 asterisks for entry should be enough */
            width = XTextWidth(planfont, prompts[i].prompt,

10625: * gtk/gtkentry.c: Changed gtk_entry_set_visibility to
            display asterisks instead of empty space when visible =
FALSE)

197:   pw->show_stars_p = get_boolean_resource("passwd.asterisks",
"Boolean");

13:   /**
* Begin masking...display asterisks (*)

1768: case '\t':
        // ignore white space before the first asterisk
            if (!fHadAsterisk) {

256:   for (i = 0; ident[i]; i++) if (ident[i] == '*') {if (id_len ==
-1) id_len = i; /* first asterisk */
        else if (dir_len == -1) {   /* Second asterisk */

658:   ;host=dynamic
        ;rfc2833compensate=yes   ; Compensate for pre-1.4 DTMF
transmission from another Asterisk machine.
                        ; You must have this turned on or DTMF
reception will work improperly.

2655: prompt: Prompt.
echo: 0 = don't echo; 1 = echo; 2 = echo with asterisks.

1976: B<Note:> an asterisk * is always converted into (.*?) regardless
of its context.
        Keep this in mind.

446:   in one <i>}~</i> <p>
        ~{* unnumbered asterisk footnote/endnote, insert
multiple asterisks
        if required <i>}~</i> <p>

130: /** How many asterisks appear in this position in table 14.19? Note
      * that more information than just indirectness is required to fully

58: /* FIXME: only show asterisks, dont use gets ! */
     fgets(localbuf, LOCALSIZE*sizeof(char), stdin);

691: <ul>
          <li>Fixed bug causing erroneous asterisks (*) to be left in a
comment definition when not followed by text</li>

214: It can be interesting for some tests to create altered files. This can be
      done by appending one or more asterisks "*" to the file name.

267: will match one or more asterisks in sequence.
      %String search

296: // Get the new string to measure its length. In normal
      // mode, we measure the text itself. In obscure mode, we
      // measure a string of n asterisks.
      wstring measure_text;
      if (_obscure_mode) {

350: //Keeping looking for parts until there are
      //no more asterisks in the wildcard string
      while (Match && ThisAsterisk < LastAsterisk)

627: /* Tack on what's after the last asterisk */
      strcpy (p, old_asterisk);

363: *   with the real wilds (encoded as A/Z)
      * - Finally the part of the mask that follows the last asterisk is
      *   reversed (byte order mirroring) and moved right after the first

11: /***
      Same as above, but with more asterisks
      All code between the "gates" will be excluded

Collaborations with the Google Poetry Robot

1. It's late

It's late. I buy DIY bonsai potato home shrines. I wish to see The World on the Internet. I might Cheat if the original painting is not framed by titles like Falcon 4 etc. My favorite food is still more secure than Windows! I hope to spend 2 nights at the Apple Store online or at any site based on Xoops 1. I dream that one day all volcanoes on Earth are shrunk to epigrams that inspire wonder and provoke a buildup of Alternatives.

2. Imagine a Night

Imagine a Night Illustrated with woodcuts and watercolors. You don't Have to knock yourself OUT to Feel the power. The Internet was originally a field of Darkness. Now it glimmers dimly in the background with layers of recurrent nodes. I might See shapes and colours printable on my Spindle Blank DVD. I hope my website is under the radar and Over the top.

3. The first person.

The first person is a relative of mine. I think this is FUNNY. My mom Calls me Brenna but my friend Leonard has recently quit using names because he thinks they are flimsy firewalls.

4. Lists.

Lists. I work at Burger King Corporation. Bill Gates was Once Arrested for switching Policies on the Use of Knowledge. I love my Mac because when I'm hungry it says Here you Are and gives me a Link to a story about a Different Kind of Blue. Menus. You never get tired of reading Commercialized Lists. I like to eat 'Cultured' items but Vows to stop rubbish-dumping at Multistorey buildings are exempt from nutrition.

5. See you later Alligator

See you later Alligator. It's still too early to commit. My cat is going into Opposition because many districts base their curriculum on areas of Special Expertise. I hope you have time to Think ahead. My favorite Word often changes depending on current errors. Adios. I enjoy Flying low over farmland in South Georgia and its associated Enterprises in India including Sinde. I learn Greek phrases and indications of Geographical origin. Thank you again for having me in your Language.

6. Winter in my Garden

Winter in my Garden is asleep and twitching softly. I saw deserted trenches and the difficult Path. I want One Of Those Days when the blank page fills up with Boeing and applicable privacy Laws are better defined. Why do I Have to make my avatar look like the second most Popular recipe from kelloggs? I never Promised to fix the roof while there's a galaxy to grow. I might See the Boom shadow falling on the Cedars.

7. George Herbert

including hardcovers
softcovers   This volume.

*

Yahoo was all aglow with love
                              's silent geometry

Further explained In terms
of the end   of the Internet

*

Across the existing doorbell chime and the presence of Noise (by?) we
should have Written about a software system with conceptual
structures

I dream   that I saw

*

two clouds
at morning Tinged
with a lovely subtle design
of alternating Logic Full of exceptions
and investigations related to Certain input
I don't Understand

Poem Method in its
Application to Quantifying technological
opportunity and thus attach the
moving portions serving
as an interim State.
Yahoo

*

was all aglow with love's
light wings   did I forget

lyrics
above?

I learn Best when information

is displayed
without   overlapping.

*

I never read Poems
like this

from George Herbert and the (architecture of) Innovations

is a network Interface

                    is a type
                    of mobile   Search

8. A dozen questions for a wise cupcake

1. O wise cupcake, Why is everyone So obsessed with the Accidental Expert?
2. O wise cupcake, is there such Thing As a Gloriously?
3. O wise cupcake! I dream to Keep my Journey to the Galapagos but did the earth rotate faster in the Early stages of Economic Evolution?
4. O wise cupcake, might you explain why coffee is so complex and Yet surprisingly fleet?
5. O wise cupcake, is there a 'Right' to (insert comma), or (insert question mark)?
6. O wise cupcake, have you ever seen A Kernel of corn pop and fall into disobedience?
7. O wise cupcake. Why do I Keep writing Poems Which start with Win dows and lights and Stuff, especially ladders?
8. O wise cupcake, how COME the settings are changeable on such diverse matters as certainty, and also 'rigor'?
9. O wise cupcake, Why is it that big Antennas don't always like Talking to the Moon?
10. o wise cupcake, are you thinking of converting everything to lower case examples?
11. O wise cupcake, has the tasty tide been Added to the Navigation?
12. O wise cupcake why don't these things Ever bloom like sunlight In The Rain?

Notes

1. The source code poems: "Stars", "No stars tonight", "Source code poems" and "Source code for the Asterisk Machine Mark 3" were created using code found via "Google Code Search": http://www.google.com/codesearch

2. The Asterisk Machine Mark 3 is the online version of a work by Bill Manhire, which was originally displayed on a three-faced rotographic display unit (The Asterisk Machine Mark 1) and also appeared in text format (The Asterisk Machine Mark 2): http://www.nzepc.auckland.ac.nz/authors/manhire/asteriskintro.asp

3. "Ernie and Bert sestina" is based on rearrangements of text found in sketch descriptions of Ernie and Bert episodes at "Muppet Wiki": http://muppet.wikia.com/wiki/Ernie_and_Bert_Sketches

4. The inspiration for "Haunted Sestina", and some of its words and phrases were found in the 1975 Standard Operating Procedure manual for Disneyland's Haunted Mansion: http://tinselman.typepad.com/tinselman/2005/08/_latest_populat.html

5. "Eye chart" was created at "Eye chart maker": http://www.eyechartmaker.com/

6. The Google Poetry Robot is found at http://www.gpeters.com/auto/autotype.php

7. "Golf Course" was created using words found in the "OneLook Reverse Dictionary": http://www.onelook.com/reverse-dictionary.html

Acknowledgements

Thank you very much to David Musgrave for publishing these poems. Thanks also to the editors of the following publications in which some of the poems first appeared:

Antipodes, Cordite, Southerly, HEAT, Turbine, Nth Position, Sport, Alba, Otoliths, Concelebratory Shoehorn Review, Mascara, Quadrant, Poetry Mosman: an anthology (River Road Press, 2008) and *All Together Now: A Digital Bridge for Auckland and Sydney* (New Zealand Electronic Poetry Centre, 2010). Some poems were first published in my chapbook *Cloud Theory* (Puncher and Wattmann, 2007).

I would like to thank the following people whose various forms of support and encouragement I have deeply appreciated: Nick Smith, Peter and Louise Vidler, Vivian and Sybille Smith, Bill Manhire, Harry and Belinda Ricketts, Nick Riemer and Gillian Sykes.

www.ingramcontent.com/pod-product-compliance
Lightning Source LLC
Chambersburg PA
CBHW031005090426
42737CB00008B/687

www.ingramcontent.com/pod-product-compliance
Lightning Source LLC
Chambersburg PA
CBHW031005090426
42737CB00008B/687